I0758693
EASTER

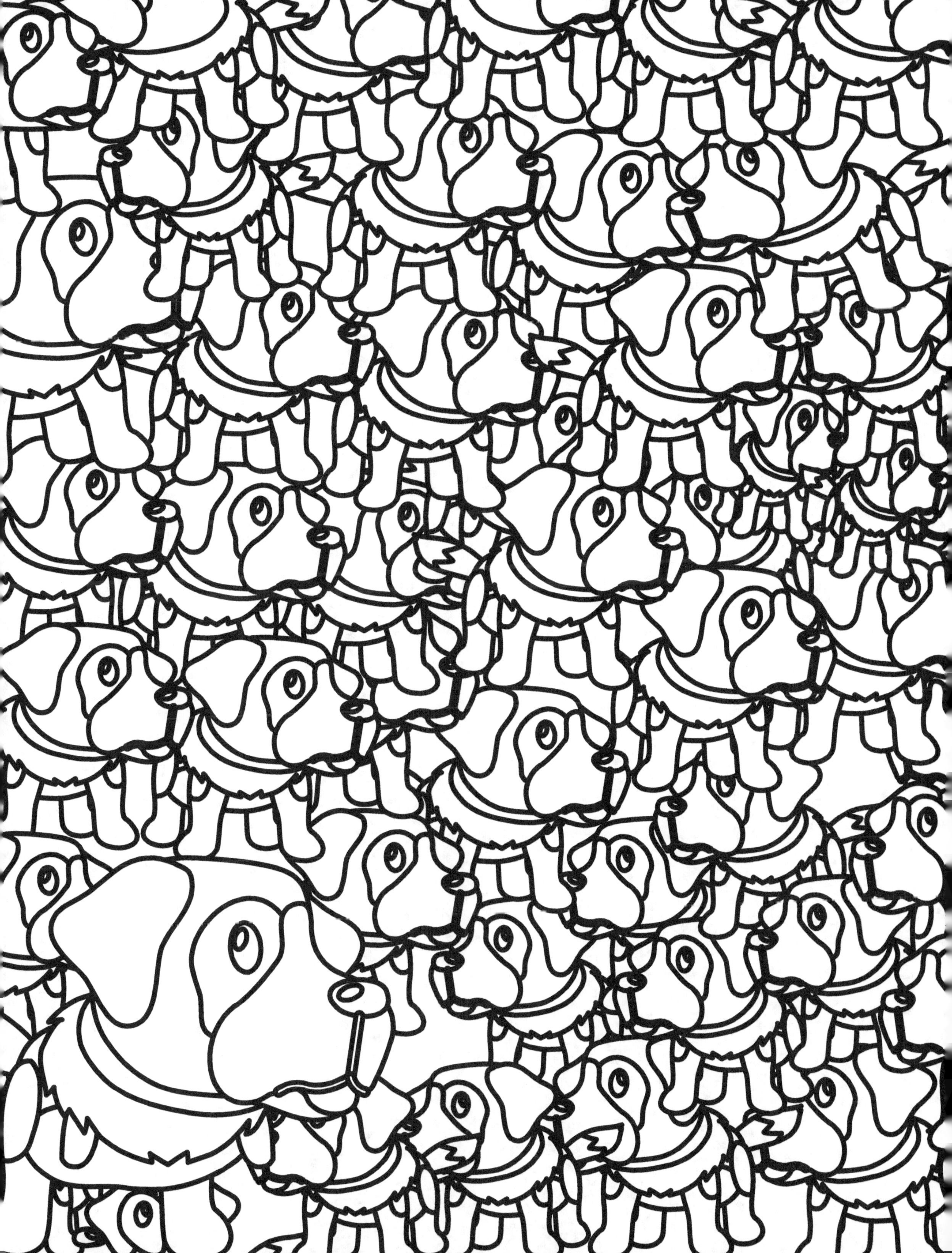

HAPPY
Easter

EASTER

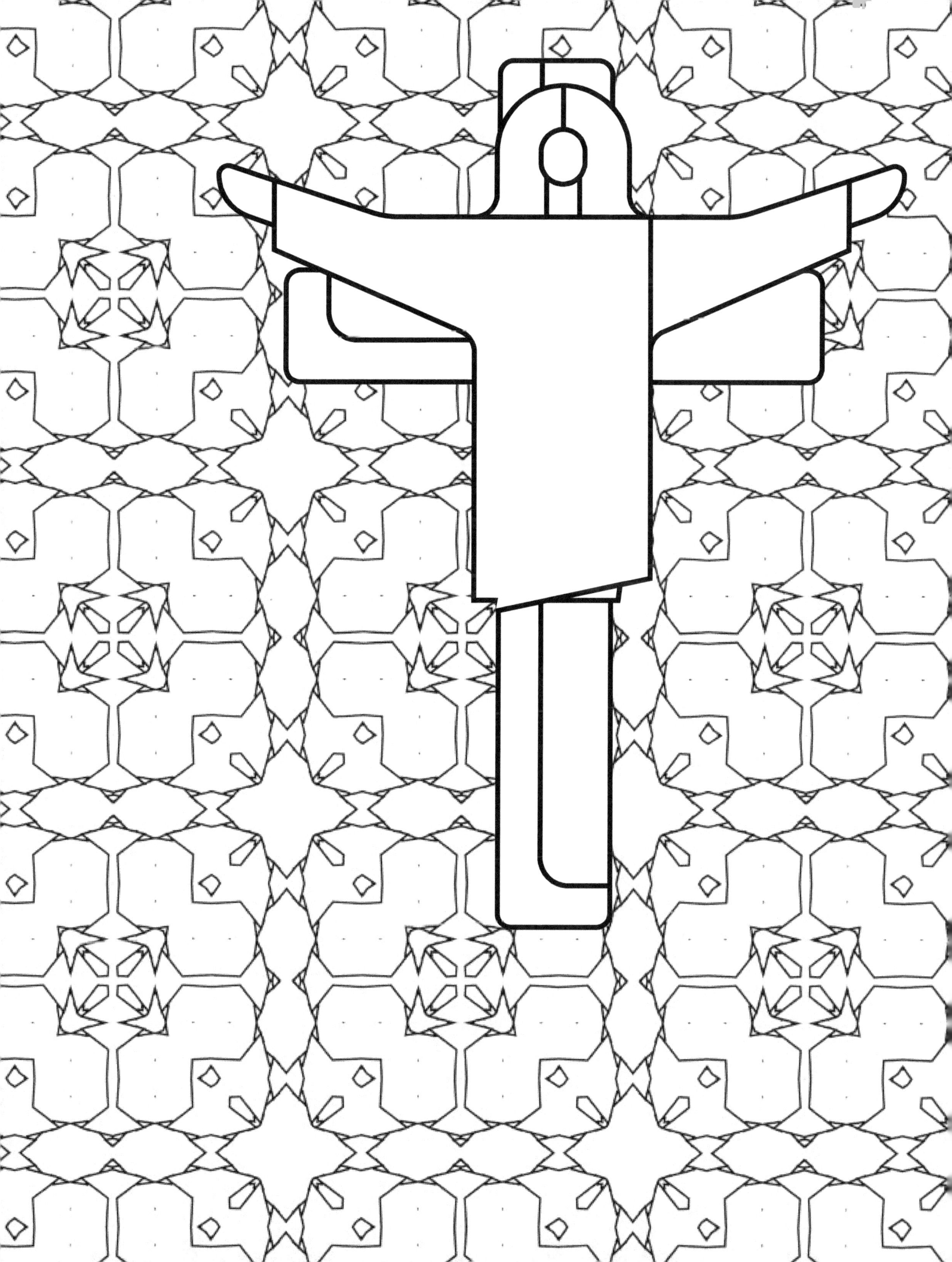

Friends
ARE THE
FAMILY
YOU
choose

STAY
Magical

Colour Crossword

What is the color of the strawberry? 1

What is the color of the carrots? 3

What is the color of the banana? 2

4 Is a berry but their color is like a deep sea?

What is the color of the spinach? 6

5 Is an exotic fruit called dragon fruit what color is?

EASTER EGG HUNT

HAPPY
Easter

HAPPY
Easter

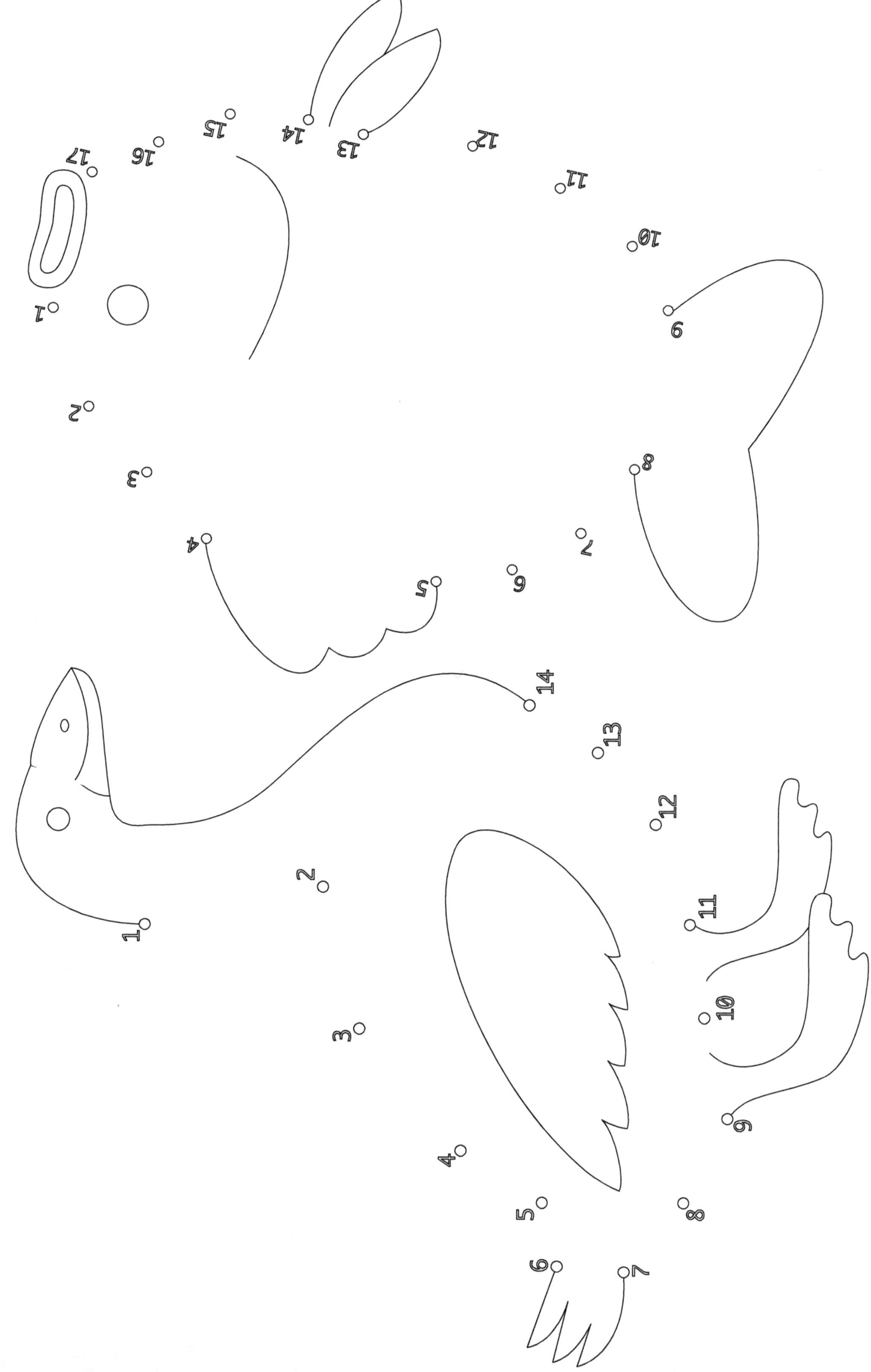

FRACTIONS

$\dfrac{2}{3}$

Green

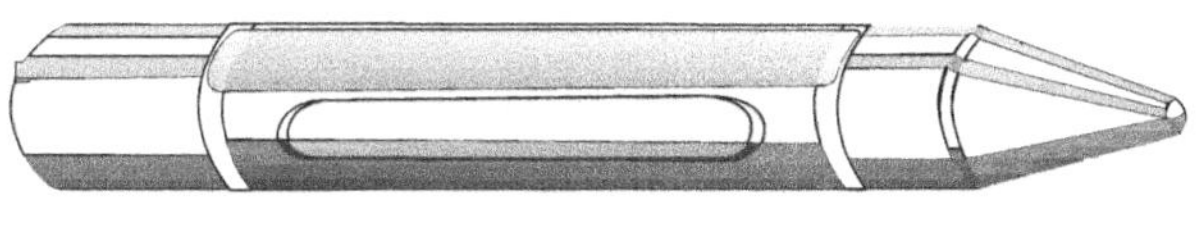

$\dfrac{3}{4}$
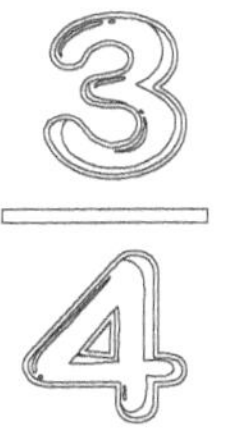

Yellow

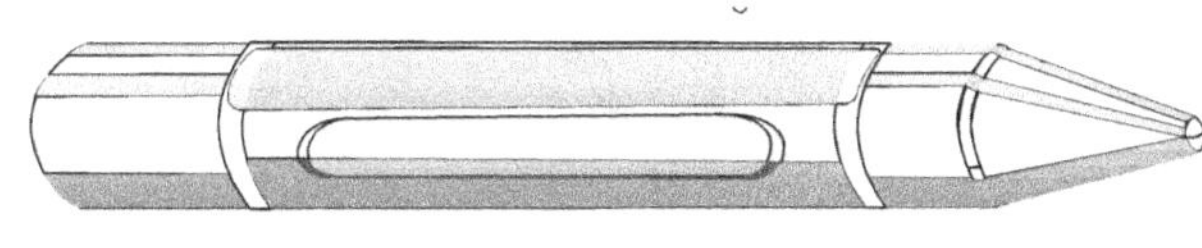

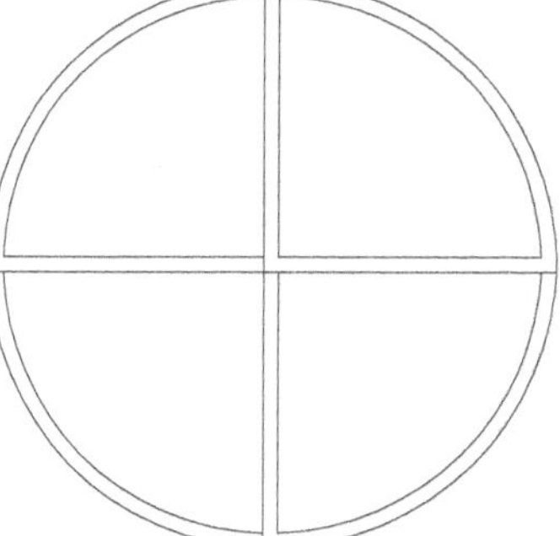

$\dfrac{2}{4}$
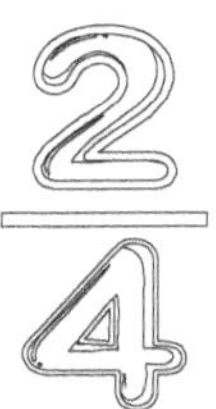

Orange

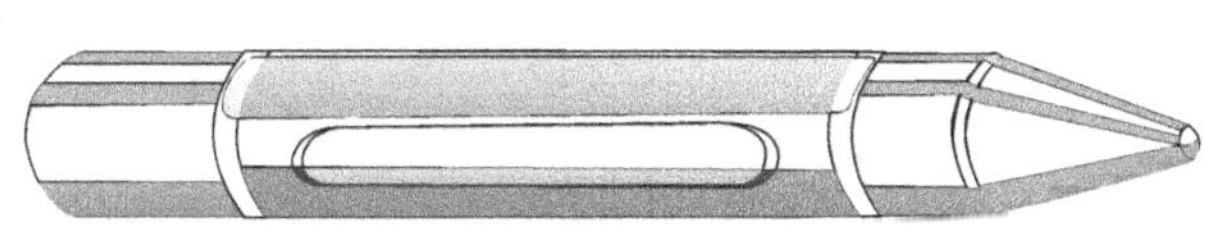

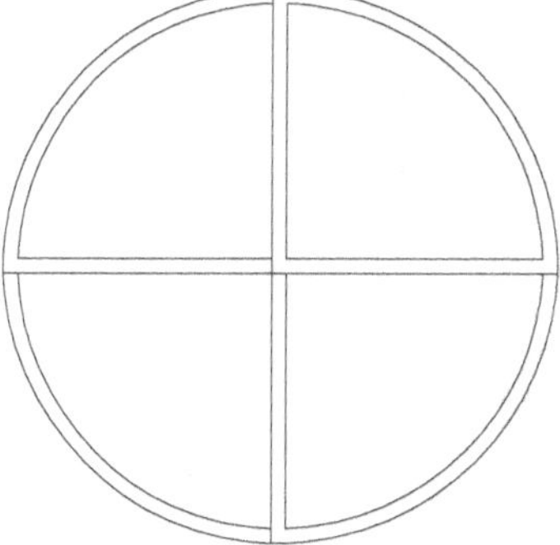

$\dfrac{1}{2}$
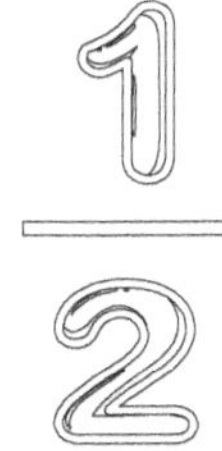

Red

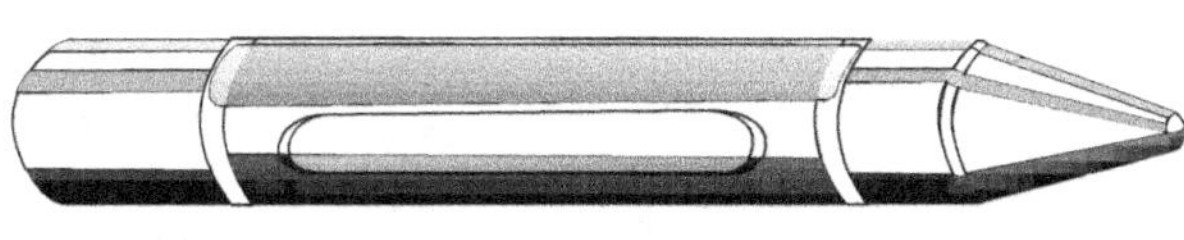

SUDOKU

8		6			3		9	
	4			1			6	8
2			8	7				5
1		8			5		2	
	3		1				5	
7		5		3		9		
	2	1			7		4	
6				2		8		
	8	7	6		4			3

E
I
A M
BRANCH
S

S
E
I
AM
RISEN

S
E
I AM
DOOR

E
S
I AM
VINE

E
S
I
AM
LIFE

E
S
I
AM
HOPE

HOW MANY EASTER EGGS
HAS THE SAME PATTERN?
COLOR EACH SET WITH
THE SAME COLORS.

Credits

Happy Easter with my cute pets, Cololring and Activity Book
First Edition 2021
©Kathia Alsina
San Juan, PR

Images, Fonts & Vector Illustrations by:

vecteezy.com
https://www.creativefabrica.com/ref/861419/

ISBN: 9798723831926

Info:
http://transformatecreando.com
Book Design and Concept by Kathia Alsina

Dedicated to

My always friend Aianna. Also to my Facebook friend
Sol Rosado and her daughters, where each post
brought me joy during this season

Solutions

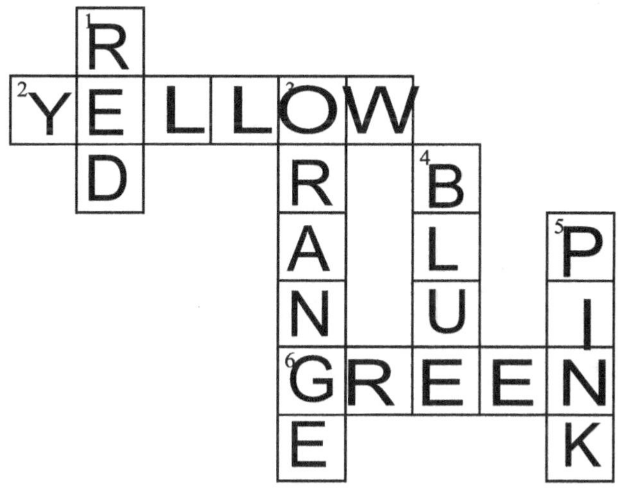

ANSWER

8	7	6	5	4	3	1	9	2
5	4	3	2	1	9	7	6	8
2	1	9	8	7	6	4	3	5
1	9	8	7	6	5	3	2	4
4	3	2	1	9	8	6	5	7
7	6	5	4	3	2	9	8	1
3	2	1	9	8	7	5	4	6
6	5	4	3	2	1	8	7	9
9	8	7	6	5	4	2	1	3